D1383862

ST DAVID
of Dewisland

Nona Rees

Illustrations: Terry John

Photographs: Aled Hughes

Gomer

New and updated edition published in 2008 by
Gomer Press, Llandysul, Ceredigion, SA44 4JL
Originally published by Gomer Press in 1992.

ISBN 978 1 84323 691 7
A CIP record for this title is available from the British Library.

Printed and bound in Wales at
Gomer Press, Llandysul, Ceredigion

I am David.
In the Vale of Roses
I have built my house
In a solitude of stones
   Crowded with daffodils
   In a cleft of sea-green hills.

I am David.
The winds of winter
Spoke to me here,
The music of water,
   The canticle of spring
   Which all the wild birds sing.

I am David.
I am the Waterman
By the banks of the river
In a vale of sweet springs
   Hidden from the sea's salt swell,
   Here I have dug my well.

I am David
I am the Dovebearer.
I speak of peace.
I counsel joy.
   In a fold of the furthest west,
   Here is my stone-ribbed nest.

I am David.
Under my feet
The rock of Dyfed
Has raised me up
   To tower in time's March gales.
   I am David. I am Wales.

Raymond Garlick

Contents

Introduction: St David – Dewi Sant   1

The Story of St David's Life   3

Dark Ages to the Reformation   13

Traditions of Dewisland:
    A Saint in the Landscape   21

St David in History,
    Tradition and Folklore   35

Epilogue   49

Bibliography   51

Index   53

Carn Llidi and Croeswdig

St David – Dewi Sant

SAINT DAVID – Dewi Sant, the patron saint of Wales, was a monk, abbot and bishop who lived in the sixth century. He was one of the many early saints who helped to revitalise and spread Christianity among the Celtic peoples of western Britain. The new faith both absorbed and replaced the worship of Celtic deities and more general concepts which included fertility and sacred kingship, nature and the universe.

St David spent a large part of his life in Mynyw, later to be called Tyddewi, St Davids. The date of his birth is not known. He died on a Tuesday, 1 March in either 589 or 601 AD, which has since been celebrated as his saint's day, *Dydd Gwyl Ddewi*. It is followed on 3 March by the saint's day of his mother, St Non. St David's body was buried in the grounds of his own monastery where the cathedral stands today.

All the traditions about the saint agree that he was tall (his height was 4 cubits – 2 metres or 6 feet) and that he was physically strong: he was able to bear a yoke and pull a plough as well as any team of oxen, yet his diet was mainly bread and herbs. A herb widely used at the time and which formed an important part of the diet of early Christian communities was watercress. Water was an important feature in the life of David: not only were major events in his life marked by the appearance of springs of water (later to become holy wells) but he was also one of several Welsh saints known as 'watermen' (*dyfrwr* in Welsh and *aquaticus* in Latin). David drank only water and, as a self-imposed penance, would stand up to his neck in cold water reciting the psalms. A medieval couplet celebrates the Waterman:

> *Dewi ddyfrwr yw'n ddiwyd*
> *Dafydd ben Sant bedydd byd.*

> (Dewi the waterman, faithful is he
> Dafydd the chief saint of Christendom).

> Ieuan ap Rhydderch, 15th century

David was attractive in appearance and was always accompanied by an angelic presence. Like all other saints, he possessed healing powers and could work miracles. The medieval church wanted to stress the ways in which the lives of the saints imitated the life of Christ. Miracles, particularly those of healing and the restoring of sight to the blind, have a literal and symbolic significance; in the words of the prophet Isaiah foretelling the coming of the Messiah:

> Then shall the eyes of the blind be opened.

David was, perhaps, the most charismatic of all the Welsh saints and from the twelfth century his cult and reputation were both national and international.

As a person, he was a mystic and an ascetic, firm in the ruling of his monastery, but a man of profound godliness, humility and perhaps reticence. He was a linguist and scholar, establishing an important teaching monastery in Mynyw which sent missionaries to Ireland, and in turn attracted holy men and women from Ireland and other Celtic lands. David spoke an early form of Welsh at a time when 'the language of the Britons' was in the process of dividing into separate Celtic languages. He would have spoken Latin and probably an early form of Irish as well.

This is David's story, told about the place where he lived and the places where his name is remembered. I have tried to preserve local folklore and also to explore recent developments in scholarship relating to the saint.

I wish to express gratitude to those who helped me in writing *St David of Dewisland*: Dean Wyn Evans, Chancellor Donald Jones, and Dr Raymond Garlick for the use of his poem. In particular, I would like to pay tribute to the encouragement, inspiration and friendship of the late Mr D W James. The suggestions from everyone who has supported my enterprise have been valuable, the errors are mine.

Nona Rees

North Bishop

The story of St David's Life

MOST of what is known about St David comes from the *Life of St David*, written around 1080-90, by Rhygyfarch, a cleric of the monastery of Llanbadarn Fawr, near Aberystwyth. Rhygyfarch was the son of Sulien, then bishop of St Davids; the learned son of a learned father. He stated that he gathered together all he could find on the life of the saint using

> the oldest manuscripts of our country, and chiefly of his [David's] own monastery. These, though eaten away along the edges and backs by the continuous gnawing of worms and the ravages of passing years, and written in the manner of the elders, have survived until now.[1]

Much of the detail of this medieval biography has to be omitted here.[2] A Welsh Life of St David, *Llyfr Ancr Llanddewi Brefi*[3] 1346, based on Rhygyfarch's original was written at Llanddewi Brefi. It is a shortened version, the style less formal; it was intended for a Welsh audience and embodies material from other sources.

St David was of noble birth, being royally descended on both sides. In Welsh, he was known as Dewi Sant (*Sant* means holy man) and other early forms of his name were Dauyd or Dewid. Both names are early borrowings from Latin and indicate that he was named by Christians with an awareness of the importance of naming, in the hope that he would have the greatest qualities of his biblical namesake. Another early form of his name is Degui and in Brittany and Cornwall he is known as Divy. David's father, named Sant, was a son of Ceredig, prince of Ceredigion and a descendant of the northern prince and conqueror, Cunedda. His mother, Non, was also of royal descent; her father was a local chieftain called Cynir and, in medieval genealogies, she was a niece of King Arthur.

Son of Prophecy

St David's birth was prophesied in the pre-Christian world by *magi* or druids, by the legendary Merlin and in the Christian world by angelic pronouncement to Patrick and Sant.

In the medieval *Life of St David*, it is recorded that St Patrick intended to found

3

a monastery in Mynyw, but was told by an angel that the place was saved for another who would be born in 30 years' time. The disappointed Patrick was then granted a vision of all Ireland, where his own mission was to be. Before the birth of David, his father, Sant, was told by an angel in a dream that he would find three treasures by the river Teifi in Ceredigion, portions of which should be set aside in the monastery of Maucan (Tŷ Gwyn near Whitesands/Porth Mawr has been suggested), for a son yet to be born: a stag, a salmon and a swarm of bees. The medieval *Life of St David* gave the treasures a Christian interpretation: the honeycomb from the hive signified wisdom, the fish foretold the ascetic way of life, and the stag, signifying the conflict of light and darkness – good and evil – symbolised the power of the Christian church over pagan, or pre-Christian belief.

A further significance of the treasures may relate to ancient Welsh land rights that reckoned the value of the land on what it produced naturally. This cannot be entirely separated from the significance of these creatures in Celtic mythology, where bees and salmon symbolise a secret wisdom from the otherworld. The salmon has been associated with holy wells and the stag was a solar symbol, signifying rebirth and healing.

Merlin's prophecy relates to David's mother, Non:

> A preacher of Ireland shall be dumb on account of an infant growing in the womb.[4]

His words refer to an incident when the pregnant Non hid in a church where Gildas was preaching (Patrick and Aelfyw or Elvis have also been considered as possibilities). Gildas found himself unable to speak while Non remained in the church, because the child in her womb would be greater than he and, traditionally, the lesser could not speak before the greater.

Birth of David

> *Santes gydles lygadlon*
> *Ei fam dda ddinam oedd Non*
> *Ferch Ynyr fawr ei chenedl,*
> *Lleian wiw, gwych ydiw'r chwedl.*

> A beneficial bright-eyed saint
> Was Non his good pure mother
> Daughter of Ynyr of great family,
> Fine nun, it is a wonderful tale.

Iolo Goch[5]

One day, when Sant was out riding, he set eyes on the beautiful Non and raped her. The resulting conception of David was marked by the appearance of two great stones, one at her head and one at her feet. When the time came for Non to

St Non's Chapel ruins

give birth, she sought out a special place. The local chieftain, Cynir, who according to medieval genealogy was Non's father, alarmed by the prophecy of 'He who will come, whose power will fill the whole land', plotted to kill Non and her unborn child, but elemental disturbance surrounded and protected her: a storm broke with 'Lightnings, thunder, floods and hail'. As Non gave birth an unearthly light, as bright as the sun, shone on the place, where all was calm and serene. In the pain of labour, Non grasped a stone which took on the imprints of her fingers, and then divided in the middle and moved to stand at her head and at her feet. At the birth of the saint, a spring of crystal water issued from the ground.

Later, the infant David was baptised by Aelfyw or Elvis, possibly his cousin, and later Bishop of Munster. A blind monk, Movi, was holding the baby when the baptismal water splashed into his eyes, and his sight was restored. Once again a spring of pure water rose from the ground. In a medieval verse:

> *Dyw wrth vedyddiaw Dewi*
> *Y wnaeth ffons oddyfwr yni*
> *Roes y Dadbedydd medd rai*
> *Y olwc gynt ny welai*

> [At the baptism of Dewi,
> God made a well for us
> Which some say,
> Gave sight to Dewi's blind godfather.]

> Ieuan ap Rhydderch

5

A typical beehive hut

David's Education

As it was with many well-born young men of the period, David's life, from infancy, was dedicated to the Church. He was taught by eminent scholars at centres of learning which cannot now be identified. The names still exist, however, and may refer to a parish, or perhaps just to a hamlet or farmstead. David's first tutor was his uncle, Gustilianus at Henfynyw (the old grove), possibly on the site of the church of that name near Aberaeron, Ceredigion. Later, David was taught by Paulinus in Carmarthenshire (possibly Whitland) and his first miracle was that of restoring the sight of his teacher.

David's Mission

His education completed, David founded monasteries at Glastonbury, Bath, Croyland, Repton, Colva, Glascwm, Leominster, Raglan and Llangyfelach. Traditions, holy wells and place-names indicate that both St David and St Non had links with Devon, Cornwall (Altarnon and Davidstowe or Dewstowe), and Brittany – St Divy, Lotivy, Brandivy and Dirinon, where St Non is said to have died. Her medieval tomb is in Dirinon church and there is a strong cult of both Non and David in the area.[6] Links with County Wexford, Ireland were also close.

A cataclysmic event during David's lifetime was the plague, or Yellow Pestilence, which struck around the year 547.[7] It resulted in a widespread evacuation of south-west Wales which may have accounted for the spread of David and Non dedications to other parts of the south-west. The climate was warmer and wetter than today and the plague was spread by water droplets from tornadoes that travelled along the swampy valley floors, sucking up and dispersing foul and stagnant water. It was said that 'whatever living creatures it touched with its pestiferous blast either immediately died or sickened for death'. Those suffering from it had a yellow or jaundiced appearance and it spared neither man nor beast.[8]

Exactly how far and for how long David travelled is not known, but he returned to Mynyw to establish his monastery. There is a local belief that the original church was built in the region of Tywyn common, above Whitesands. The earliest name was Cille Muine,[9] Irish words for the (monastic) 'cell of the grove', whence came Mynyw, the first Welsh name of David's settlement. The building work was constantly disrupted: the foundations and walls built by day were mysteriously destroyed by night, and with great noise.[10] Finally David was warned by the angel who was to accompany him throughout his life, not to build there but to build in *Vallis Rosina* or Glyn Rhosyn, the valley of the little marsh. It is known today simply as 'the valley'.

David and Boia

David came to Glyn Rhosyn with three followers, Aeddan, Ismael and Teilo, all important Welsh saints – Teilo was to succeed David as Bishop of Mynyw. Here, on this western peninsula, Christianity had its last conflict with the old religion.

Boia, Irishman and druid, was a chieftain of some standing. One day he looked down from his fortified settlement on Clegyr Boia and, to his dismay, saw the smoke of a fire swirling over the valley. The fire, lit by David and his companions, was a ritual proclamation of his ascendancy and power. The smoke covered 'the whole island and Ireland'. The valley may have been a sacred place long before the coming of Christianity, and the river Alun[11] may have been named after a Celtic river deity, Alauna. A struggle ensued which divided itself into three episodes, suggesting a ritualised confrontation.

Clegyr Boia

Boia was urged on by a determined wife to send his warriors against David. Tradition has named her Satrapa, but this was a mistranslation of the Latin word for chieftain and would have referred to Boia. David countered with a 'spell' that caused Boia's men and cattle to fall down as if dead. Boia then came to terms with David, granting him the land and even becoming a convert, and the spell was lifted. Boia's wife, however, continued her opposition and sent her maidens to bathe naked in the river Alun. This was not only to try the monastic vows of abstinence, but it may also have had further ritual significance. The monks begged David to leave, but he replied, 'No, we shall stay, it is Boia who must go.' Finally, in a third act against David, Boia's wife lured her innocent and trusting stepdaughter Dunod down to the valley to gather hazel nuts. She made Dunod lay her head in her stepmother's lap so that she might examine (or dress) her hair, and then cut off the girl's head.[12] As with so many events involving birth and death, water – the ancient symbol of rebirth and the life force – sprang from the ground. The well so-created was revered in Norman times and the place called Merthyr Dunod, the grave of Dunod the Martyr, but its whereabouts is unknown.

At this martyrdom, all opposition to David was overcome. Boia's wife became mad and disappeared. Boia, evidently demoralised and undoubtedly grief-stricken, started to plot against David again. Early one morning, Boia's camp was left undefended and another Irishman called Lisci landed at Porth Lisci (Lisci's harbour), stormed the camp and beheaded Boia. The account described how 'fire fell from heaven' and destroyed everything.

Life in a Celtic Monastery

David's settlement in the valley would have been a simple one, consisting of circular huts, an oratory and preaching crosses, and all surrounded by a wall. Nothing of this survives today, although a church would have stood on the site until the first Norman cathedral was built in 1131. Rhygyfarch gives a vivid account of early monastic life. The day began with prayer followed by labour in the fields using mattocks, spades, hoes and saws for cutting. Oxen were not used: the monks pulled the plough, bearing the yoke on their shoulders. When these tasks were finished, the monks returned to reading, writing or prayer. At the sound of the bell they went to church to chant psalms and pray 'until stars are seen in the heaven bringing the day to a close'. A simple supper, generally consisting of bread and herbs, was followed by three further hours of prayer, after which the monks slept till cockcrow. Daily tasks also involved caring for the sick, the needy and the pilgrim. Clothing was of 'mean quality, mainly skins'. All property was held in common; it was customary for families of men entering a monastery to make gifts of land to the monastic establishment concerned, but David did not accept such gifts from those entering his own monastery which imposed a particularly challenging novitiate.

The Pilgrimage to Jerusalem

David was directed by an angel to make a pilgrimage to Jerusalem. With two saintly companions, Teilo and Padarn, he set out for the Holy Land. David was endowed with the gift of tongues and acted as interpreter. An index of early bardic lore, preserved in a collection of sayings – *Trioedd Ynys Prydein (The Triads of the Isle of Britain)*[13] – called them the 'three Blessed Visitors of the Isle of Britain'. At Jerusalem, they had audience with the Patriarch who consecrated David as Archbishop and presented them with four gifts: a bell, a staff, a tunic woven with gold and an altar.

The Synod of Brefi

The event that placed David first among the bishops of western Britain, giving all churches dedicated to him supreme rights of sanctuary, took place at Llanddewi Brefi (the church of David on the Brefi stream), in the remote and wooded hill country of Ceredigion, *circa* 545.

A meeting (or synod) of churchmen and the people had been called to denounce Pelagianism, a doctrine regarded as heresy. Pelagius, a fourth-century Irish monk living in Rome, had denied the Church's teaching that a man was born in sin and redeemed by Christ. He taught that man was responsible for his own sin and therefore, by his own efforts, his own salvation. This teaching caused much anxiety amongst Church leaders and so the synod was

Frederick Mancini's sculpture
at Llanddewi Brefi

Llanddewi Brefi

held. At first, little progress was made, so Paulinus, David's early teacher, urged that David, who was not present, should be brought to speak. When first approached, David was doubtful of his ability to convince the multitude when such a learned assembly had failed. He was persuaded finally by two leading churchmen, Deiniol (Bishop of Bangor) and Dyfrig, or Dubricius, traditionally Archbishop of Caerleon.

On the way to Brefi, one of David's acclaimed miracles took place: he restored life to the dead child of a widow. A spring, Ffynnon Ddewi, near the church, marked the site. The child followed David to Brefi as a young disciple. When David reached Brefi, he ascended a mound of garments, spread a 'handkerchief',[14] or napkin on the ground on which he stood to preach. With clarity and conviction, David denounced the heresy; as he spoke, the ground rose higher under him to form a hill and a snow-white dove settled on his shoulder. The white dove is a symbol of the Holy Spirit and David is usually depicted with a dove on his shoulder. From this point on, David's fame and reputation grew. A second synod assembled called the Synod of Victory, which confirmed the decrees of the Synod of Brefi.[15]

Miracles

David performed many miracles in his lifetime, bringing health to the sick and dying and confounding the treachery of those who would poison him. After his death, prayers of the faithful continued to produce miracles, including rescue from injury, shipwreck and imprisonment. During the Middle Ages, miracles were of great importance in establishing the cult and importance of saints and encouraging pilgrimage to their shrines.[16]

The Death of David

David died in old age, having acquired the image of earlier Celtic heroes and gods, including a legendary life-span of 147 years. His 'birthday in heaven' was faithfully remembered as Tuesday, 1 March, when the monastery was filled with angels.

Notes

1 Rhygyfarch *Life of St David.*

2 Two texts are used: BM ms Vespasian A iv., now believed to be the earliest extant version of Rhygyfarch's *Life of St David* was chosen by A. W. Wade-Evans for his *Life of St David,* SPCK, 1923, and BM ms Nero E was translated by I. J. W. James, University of Wales, Cardiff, 1983.

3 *The Welsh Life of St David* ed. D. Simon Evans, Cardiff University Press, 1988.

4 *The History of the Kings of Britain* Geoffrey of Monmouth, Penguin Classics, 1966.

5 *Iolo Goch Poems,* ed. Dafydd Johnston, Gomer Press, 1993.

6 Yves de Berre, Bernard Tanguy, Yves-Pascal Castel, *Buez Santes Nonn, Mystere Breton. Vie de Sainte Nonna,* 2000, gives a full, illustrated account of the church at Dirinon and its history in French and Breton.

7 *The Anglo Saxon Chronicle,* James Ingram (trns.), Everyman Press, 1912.

8 *Book of Llandaf, Life of Teilo,* 343 Welsh MSS Soc., 1840

9 *Chronicum Scotorum,* ed. W. M. Hennessy, 1866; I. B. G. Charles *Place-names of Pembrokeshire* NLW, 1992.

10 Told to author by Mr Edwin Morris, late of Porth Mawr and Croeswdig.

11 George Owen and Richard Fenton spell it *Alan.*

12 Evidence of human sacrifice among Celtic tribes is to be found in contemporary accounts by Roman writers such as Tacitus (*Annals XIV xxix-xxx*) and archaeological discoveries, for example the bog bodies found at Lindow Moss, Cheshire, and at Tollund, Denmark. Sacrifice of this nature had great ritual significance and would probably only be used when the tribe or territory was threatened. Human sacrifice was also carried out at the foundation of a building and, on occasions, this has been uneasily absorbed into the folklore concerning the establishment of some early Christian monasteries. There is a suggestion here of ritual sacrifice overlaid by Christian tradition.

13 Triad 82 in *Trioedd Ynys Prydein, The Welsh Triads,* Rachel Bromwich, University of Wales Press, 1978.

14 Vespasian text only.

15 Synod of Victory 569, *Annales Cambriae* Rolls Series, 1908.

16 A collection of the posthumous miracles of St David has been translated by M. J. Curley *Eleven Miracles of St David* (BL MS Royal 13 Ci), University of Puget Sound. *Traditio* Vol 62, 2007.

Dark Ages to the Reformation

THE original monastic church founded by St David was destroyed by fire in 645 AD,[1] and successive settlements suffered much from Norse raids. Bishop Bernard built the first Norman cathedral on the same site in 1131. It was taken down and rebuilt in 1181 as it stands today, by Bishop Peter de Leia.

The first recorded mention of St David occurred in the *Catalogus Sanctorum Hiberniae*, a catalogue of the saints of Ireland, dated to the ninth or tenth centuries, but referring to an earlier list of saints, dated 544-598. The earliest liturgical mention of St David occurs in another Irish list of saints, the *Martyrology of Tallaght*, dated before the year 800.[2] This records that the second order of saints in Ireland received a rite of Mass 'from the holy men of Britain, St David, St Gildas and St Docus [Cadog]'.

From earliest times, David's monastery appears to have been a centre of learning. The *Life of St David* makes reference to the copying of books such as the Gospels and the Psalter, and the medieval cathedral library had a wealth of richly illuminated manuscripts which were destroyed at the Reformation and during the Civil War. One early manuscript, written at St Davids, was the *Liber Davidis* (Book of David), a penitential ascribed to St David and now only known from extracts in a manuscript preserved in Paris.[3] Another was the *Evangelium*, an illuminated manuscript of St John's Gospel, written by St David himself 'in letters of gold'.

In Wales, the earliest existing reference to St David is at Llanddewi Brefi, Ceredigion. In 1693, Welsh antiquary Edward Lhuyd discovered a gravestone in the wall of the church, with the following inscription: '*Hic iacet Idnert Filius Jacobi qui occisus fuit propter predam Sancti David*' (Here lies Idnert, son of Jacobus who was killed defending the church of the Holy David from despoliation).[4] The inscription is early seventh-century and is an almost contemporary reference to the saint. Two fragments survive, used as building stones on the external west wall of the church, and what remains of the script is well preserved.

David's name was found in the Calendars of Glastonbury and Sherborne (Wessex), his fame possibly spread by Asser, a bishop of St Davids and King Alfred's biographer. His name appears in the tenth-century Salisbury psalter.[5] *Canu i Dewi*[6] a poem by the medieval Welsh poet Gwynfardd Brycheiniog (*c.*

1170) listed all the Dewi churches of the time. Eventually some 53 churches were dedicated to St David in South Wales and the border, though none in north Wales.

In 1123, in the episcopate of Bernard, the first Norman bishop (1115-1146), David was officially recognised by Pope Callistus II, who dedicated the cathedral to St Andrew and St David and granted the concession that two pilgrimages to St Davids equalled one to Rome.[7] In Latin, it read:

Roma semel quantum, bis dat Menevia tantum

and in Welsh a rhyme summarised it neatly:

Dos i Rufain unwaith
ac i Fynyw ddwywaith
A'r un elw cryno
a gei di yma ag yno.

This recognition meant that St Davids became one of the most important pilgrim shrines in Britain, visited by William the Conqueror in 1081,[8] Henry II in 1171 and 1172,[9] Edward I and Queen Eleanor in 1284[10] and Richard II in 1394.[11] Edward I acquired the head of St David on his visit to Wales[12] and an armbone of the saint was found among his effects after his death.[13] St Davids is one of only three places in Wales marked on the *Mappa Mundi* in Hereford Cathedral, the great medieval map of pilgrimage (*c* 1300) that places Jerusalem as the centre of the known world. By the time Rhygyfarch wrote his late twelfth-century *Life*, David's reputation was becoming well established: he was the only purely Welsh saint formally enrolled in the calendars of the western Church.

Inscribed stone 'OCCISI' (OCCISUS), Llanddewi Brefi.

14

Medieval shrine of St David, Presbytery.

The body of St David was buried in his own monastery though where is not known. The relics of the saint preserved by the Welsh church would have been such items as his hand bell, the Gospel of St John, written in the saint's own hand, his staff and perhaps items of clothing. In the eighth century, Glastonbury claimed 'the blessed David' as its chief patron after Our Lady. In the tenth century, the relics of St David were claimed to be in the possession of Glastonbury, where he established a church.[14]

In the ninth and tenth centuries, St Davids suffered much from Viking raids[15] and in the eleventh century, the tomb of the saint was reported to be very overgrown.[16] The Welsh kings, Rhys ap Tewdwr and Gruffudd ap Cynan, swore an oath of friendship on the relics of St David, before they fought and won the Battle of Mynydd Carn (Pembrokeshire) in 1081.[17] In 1089, however, the shrine was stolen and plundered of its rich ornaments and the site of David's grave was forgotten. In the thirteenth century, it was revealed to the Prior of Ewenni, John de Gamages, in a dream that St David's body was buried outside the south porch of the cathedral. The Prior's instructions, as given in his dream, were followed to the letter and excavations revealed the body of the saint.[18]

In 1275, Bishop Richard de Carew built a new shrine on the north side of the presbytery. Three figures were painted on the shrine: St David, St Patrick and an unnamed saint ('somewhat defac'd'), possibly St Stinan,[19] friend and confessor to St David. A *feretrum* or portable shrine would have been kept, housing the bones of St David and carried around the country by chantry priests, accompanied by the bishop's tenants, invoking the saint's aid in guarding his ancient realm. In time of war, the *feretrum* would be carried ahead of the army.[20]

Cross, City Square.

16

In 1398, Archbishop of Canterbury, Roger Walden, elevated the feast day of St David to a status meriting a service of nine lessons and in 1415, Archbishop Chichele, previously bishop of St Davids, decreed a full choral setting for the service.[21] It was not until the sixteenth century, however, that David became recognised as the patron saint of Wales.

In 1969, a handsome oak-bound antiphonal, the Pen Pont Antiphoner, containing words and music for use at vespers and matins for St David's Day, was acquired by the National Library of Wales at Aberystwyth. It is the only surviving source for the offices for St David's feast day in use before the Reformation. It dates from the mid-fourteenth century. The layout follows the Sarum rite which would have been used in the cathedral. The vigil for the feast day would start with vespers at 5.00 pm on the last day of February, and matins would be sung at 3.00 am on 1st March, in a cathedral dimly lit by lamps and candles. The readings would have included excerpts from the *Life of St David*.[22]

At the Reformation, the Protestant Bishop Barlow seized the relics which consisted of 'two heads of silver plate enclosing two rotten skulls stuffed with putrified cloutes, two arm bones and a worm-eaten book covered with silver plate'.[23] These would have been destroyed as both Welsh and pilgrim devotion ensured that such veneration would be ruthlessly stamped out. The religious festival ceased and in 1550, the destruction of the cathedral service books by Bishop Ferrar was lamentably thorough. Nevertheless, it was unusual for so much of a primary shrine to have survived the Reformation, possibly due to the close presence of the tomb of Owain Tudor, grandfather of Henry VIII, moved from the Greyfriars church, Carmarthen at the Reformation.

In the nineteenth century, during cathedral restoration by Sir Gilbert Scott, building work uncovered the recess in the west wall of Holy Trinity Chapel, revealing bones embedded in mortar, lying on the sill. They were reinterred beneath the floor and recovered early in the 20th century by Dean Williams who was convinced that these were the bones of St David, although at the time (*c* 1920) this belief was not entirely shared by the Chapter or by St Davids itself. St David is a major saint in the Orthodox Church and in 1925, the cathedral was presented with the reliquary for the bones by the Orthodox Patriarchs. In 1996, a selection of these bones was carbon-dated at Oxford by Professor Bernard Knight; in March 1997 the results were made public in two Independent Television programmes. The tests revealed that the earliest bone was twelfth-century and others gave thirteenth-, fourteenth- and nineteenth-century readings.[24]

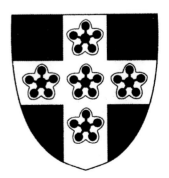

The Coat of Arms borne by the bishops and diocese of St Davids consists of a gold (or) cross on a black (sable) background and on the cross are five black cinquefoils. The cinquefoil is said to represent the Burnet rose, once known in

Bishop's Palace.

Pembrokeshire as St David's rose.[25] The origins of the Coat of Arms are obscure; it may have been that of Bishop Bernard in the early twelfth century. The colours were those of Rhys ap Tewdwr, king of south Wales when Rhygyfarch wrote his *Life of St David*. Rhys gave the Cantref of Pebidiog (the area latterly known as Dewisland) to the Church; he was killed in a skirmish in the Brecon area in 1091. In a book of pedigrees *circa* 1560, St David's Coat of Arms is described as *Dewi Fabsant*.[26]

The fame of St David and his shrine reached a high point in the Middle Ages. This is reflected in the building of the Bishop's Palace, the work of Bishop Henry de Gower (1328-47). The gracious ruins only hint at its former splendour. A wall-walk above the arcaded parapet provided wide views of the surrounding countryside. From here, liveried trumpeters would herald the arrival of distinguished guests. The palace is adorned by colourful mosaic-work, the glorious 'wheel-window' and around the walls, an exotic collection of carved heads representing God's creation from the animal kingdom to man at its head.

Notes

1 *Annales Cambriae* (Harleian). J. Ingram, The Anglo Saxon Chronicle, 1912.

2 Catalogus sanctorum Hiberniae Haddan and Stubbs, Councils, ii. 292; S. M. Harris, *Saint David in the Liturgy* University of Wales Press, 1940.

3 D. Dumville, *Saint David of Wales* (Kathleen Hughes Memorial Lectures on Mediaeval Welsh History, University of Cambridge, 2001); W. Wade-Evans, *Vitae Sanctorum Britanniae et Genealogiae* Cardiff University Press, 1944.

4 G. Griffiths, H. P. Owen, K. Jackson. 'The earliest mention of St David?' *Bulletin of the Board of Celtic Studies*, Vol. XIX, Pt III, Nov. 1961.

5 S. M. Harris, *op cit*.

6 M. E. Owen, 'Prologomena to a study of the historical context of Gwynfardd Brycheiniog's 'Poem to Dewi', *Studia Celtica*, Vol 16/27, 1991-92.

7 William of Malmesbury, *History of the English Kings, Vol 1*. R. A. B. Mynors, R. M. Thomson, M. Winterbottom, Oxford, 1998.

8 *Brut y Tywysogion*, Rolls Series, 1860.

9 *Ibid*.

10 *Annales Cambriae*, Rolls Series, 1860.

11 N. Saul, *Richard II* (Yale English Monarchs Series), Yale University Press, 1997.

12 *Chronicle of Bury St Edmunds 1212-1301*, A. Grandsdon (ed.), 1964.

13 'Edward I placed a relic of St David on the high altar of the Church of Great St Helen, and in the inventory of the king's effects taken after his death...is a casket containing brachium sancti David', note 347, Royal Commission on Ancient Monuments, Pembrokeshire, 1925.

14 J. P. Carley, *Glastonbury Abbey*, Guild Publishing, 1988.

15 *Brut y Tywysogion*, T. Jones, Cardiff University of Wales Press, 1955.

16 G. C. G. Thomas, 'A lost manuscript of Thomas Saint', *National Library of Wales Journal XXIV*, 1966.

17 *Annales Cambriae*.

18 F. G. Cowley 'A note on the discovery of St David's Body', British Board of Celtic Studies, 1960.
F. G. Cowley *St David Cult Church and Nation* 2007.

19 Memoirs relating to the Cathedral-Church of St David's and the Country adjacent, as it was in the latter End of Queen Elizabeth's Reign.

20 Browne Willis, *Survey of the Cathedral Church of St Davids*, 1717.

21 Black Book of St David's, BM Add. MSS No. 34, 125. Hon. Soc. Cymmrodorion, 1902.

22 S. M. Harris, *op cit*; S. Harper *Music in Welsh Culture before 1650: a study of the principal sources*, Ashgate, 2006/7; *St David of Wales: Cult, Church and Nation*, Boydell, 2007.

23 Owain Tudor Edwards, *Matins, Lauds and Vespers for St David's Day: The mediaeval Office of the Welsh Patron Saint.* NLW MS 20541E. D. S. Brewer, Cambridge, 1990. A reconstruction was broadcast in 1987, by the Clerkes of Oxenford, directed by David Wulstan. An excerpt from the Penpont Antiphoner Lucescente nouo mane is included in the CD *Let all the world in every corner sing!* by St Davids Cathedral Singers, directed by Simon Pearce.

24 *St David of Wales: Cult, Church and Nation*, eds. J. Wyn Evans & Jonathan M. Wooding, Boydell, 2007: 'AMS radiocarbon dating of bones from St David's cathedral' by T. F. G. Higham, C. Bronk Ramsey and L. M. Nokes.

25 R. Freethy, *From Agar to Zenry: A book of plant uses, names and folklore*, Crowood Press, 1985.

26 J. Fisher, 'The Welsh Calendar. The festivals philologically and historically treated with an account of the Gwyl Mabsant or Patronal Festival', Hon. Soc. Cymmrodorion, May 1985; British Remains 37, 1777.

19

Carn Llidi

Traditions of Dewisland:

A saint in the landscape[1]

s early as 588 AD, St Davids was known to the Irish as Cille Muine – 'the monastic cell of the grove'. In the ninth century it was called Mynyw, an old Welsh word for a bramble bush or grove. By the eleventh century it had become Latinized to Menevia. Then at the end of the fifteenth century it was referred to as Tyddewi and is still known as such today.

The valley where the cathedral stands was known by the Welsh name Hoddnant, the quiet or pleasant valley. Another Welsh name for it was Glyn Rhosyn, marshy valley, which was mistranslated into Latin as Vallis Rosina and incorrectly referred to by Giraldus Cambrensis as Valley of Roses. The river Alun, which runs past the cathedral, rises in Llandigige and reaches the sea at Porth Clais (pronounced locally as 'Claesh'). Although *clais* can mean a river valley in Welsh (like *ria*), here it is likely to mean the harbour of the monastery, from an old word *clas*: a monastic community.

In earlier times it was much easier to travel by sea than by land. St Davids lies where major sea routes running north/south and east/west (Bristol Channel to Ireland) intersect. Also, three land routes dating back to prehistoric times converged on St Davids, reaching the sea at Porth Mawr or Whitesands, the nearest point to south-west Ireland, 45 miles (64 km) away. The pilgrim paths of the Middle Ages followed these ancient trackways. Thus St Davids was at the hub of much activity and in contact with other Celtic lands, the continent and the countries of the Mediterranean.

On this peninsula Irish influence increased around the year 400 AD, with a major influx of the Deisi tribe who had been dispossessed of their lands in the area that is now Co Wexford. The ancient, royal house of Dyfed is said to have been descended from the Deisi. Most of the action of this story takes place in Dyfed, a Dark Age kingdom comprising Pembrokeshire with part of Carmarthenshire and Ceredigion.[2] The boundary of the St Davids peninsula runs from Newgale to Fishguard. In the twelfth century it was known as Pebidiog, the territory of Pebid, possibly a local overlord. By the thirteenth century it had acquired the anglicised name of Dewisland.[3]

St Non's[4]

> Here there is holy water
> Old stone and a sky
> That is timeless.
>
> R S Thomas

More than one site is claimed for the birthplace of St David.[5] The local site lies on a clifftop where a dark line of cliffs turns west into the setting sun, towards the islands of Ramsey (Ynys Dewi) and Grassholm (Gwales) and is marked by a small, ruined chapel standing in the middle of a field, dating from before 1335. The foundations may be early and what remains of the walls is medieval. The chapel faces north/south, not east/west as would be normal with Christian churches. The simple cross-inscribed stone in the south-east corner, which dates from between the seventh and the ninth century, was once built into the wall. An incomplete Bronze Age stone circle surrounds the site.[6] The chapel was abandoned before 1557 and after this date it was used as a dwelling house and the surrounding land as a leek garden.

Cross-inscribed stone, St Non's

St Non's Well

Like so many places where early Christian chapels are sited on or near prehistoric remains, St Non's has a holy well whose waters sprang from the ground at a momentous event, in this case the birth of St David. The earliest description of the well is by Browne Willis in 1715:

> There is a fine Well . . . cover'd with a stone roof, and inclos'd within a Wall, with Benches to sit upon round the Well. Some old simple people go stil to visit this Saint at some particular Times, especially on St Nun's Day (March 3) which they keep holy and offer Pins, Pebbles etc. at this well.

By 1764 the stone roof had disappeared. At some point in the late eighteenth or early nineteenth century, a domed head was put on the well by Mrs Williams of Treleddyn.[7] The present cover dates from a restoration in 1951. The footings of a stone structure in the field adjacent to the well suggest that there may have been a well chamber and associated buildings, characteristic of many medieval holy wells. Babies used to be dipped in the well, and before the Reformation its water was taken to the cathedral, consecrated and used as holy water. It is a healing well and its waters have been used to cure diseases of the eye and rheumatism. The well has an unbroken tradition of pilgrimage and healing, rooted in traditions thousands of years old.

St Non's Well

Llanon, near Llanrhian

There was an old chapel in the small hamlet of Llanon. A stone beneath the altar, said to have been brought there from St Non's, bore incised Ogham markings,[8] said to been the imprint of Non's fingers as she gave birth to David. Both chapel and stone have disappeared. The same tradition also exists at St Non's.

Nun Street, St Davids

This was originally the main road into St Davids from the north, traditionally called after St Non. The earliest reference is 1606, when it was referred to in a will as St Nunnes Streete.[9] Browne Willis (1715), refers to it as St Nuns-Street.

Porth Clais and the baptism of David

If you follow the coast path from St Non's to the ancient harbour of Porth Clais, you will come to the site of David's baptism. A chapel once stood at the head of the harbour which was called Capel y Pistyll,[10] chapel of the water spout. The chapel site and remains of its holy well are now buried deep in a thicket on private land. In the 1950s it was tended by a former cathedral verger, Mr Bill Morris. The water ran from a cowl-shaped well head through a little stone channel into a stone basin. Browne Willis described the old chapel as having a spring, or water spout, running under it 'into a cistern at ye east under ye pinion or gable of ye building'.

The Chapel of Our Lady and St Non[11]

This little chapel, near the Retreat House, was built in 1934 and modelled on the medieval chapels of which footings, ruins and restorations can be found all round the shores of Wales. Sometimes they are called reception chapels, where pilgrims would leave offerings and say prayers for a safe journey or give thanks for safe arrival. In the quiet of this little chapel, solid stone walls silence the sea and the sense of peace is profound. The altar is a composite of medieval stonework and above it a fine stained-glass window of the William Morris school depicts the arrival of St Non and the child David in Brittany. St David is also depicted in a south-facing window. The holy-water stoup to the left of the door was from Capel y Gwrhyd (Chapel of the Fathom, see opposite). The *Piscina* to the right of the altar was recovered from Caerforiog.

Chapel of Our Lady and St Non

Capel y Gwrhyd, Chapel of the Fathom

St David's legendary height was reflected in the naming of this chapel. The Welsh words *gŵr* and *hyd* translate as 'the length of a man' from which is derived the word *gwrhyd* meaning a fathom – the nautical measurement of 6 feet (2m). It was said to have been the span of David's outstretched arms as shown in a painting of him above the chancel arch, or possibly referring to the breadth of the arch itself. The chapel was sited in a field near Gwrhyd Mawr and is marked on the John Speed Map of

Gwrhyd Holy Water Stoup

1610. The names have survived at Rhodiad y Brenin, a mile from St Davids, where both Gwrhyd Mawr and Gwrhyd Bach can be found. The holy water stoup in the Chapel of Our Lady and St Non came from Capel y Gwrhyd, one key stone has also survived and a *piscina* has been seen on the site.

Yr Hen Eglwys – The Old Church

To the south and east of Whitesands Bay lies Tywyn Common or the Burrows. Beneath sands piled high by Atlantic storms may lie the site of David's first church, where his attempts to build met with failure until, warned by an angel not to build there, he moved to the Valley. This is a common theme in the folklore of many countries relating to the founding of churches and monasteries. There has been a local tradition of a Roman Station on the sandhills. In about 1539, John Leland described Whitesands and writes of a 'castel' in the area 'but the tokens be not very evidente'. Roman coins have been found on Whitesands, however, and archaeological evidence of a Roman road from the east moves ever nearer St Davids.

Porth Lisci

Porth Lisci (Lisci's Harbour) is a small beach, accessible by footpath only, on the remote south-west tip of the peninsula. Lisci was the Irish raider who killed Boia. Looking inland, the outcrop of Clegyr Boia dominates the skyline.

Headland and Island, Moorland and Mountain

The name of St David is associated with other places situated around the westernmost tip of the peninsula. The headland jutting out into a wild, offshore tide race, named *Octapitarum Promontorium* (promontory of the eight perils) by the second-century geographer Ptolemy, is known today as St David's Head or Penmaen Dewi. Nearby is Ramsey Island; an older name for the island, still used by a passing generation, is Ynys Dewi (Dewi's Island). The earliest name for Ramsey is Ynys Tyfanog (St Dyfanog's Island).[12] There were two medieval chapels on the island, one south of the farmhouse dedicated to St Stinan, and one to the north to St Tyfanog. No remains are visible.

Tŷ Gwyn, a farmhouse on the lower slopes of Carn Llidi (often called Carn Llaethdy meaning 'dairy' after a farm on its eastern slope), was the site of an early monastery, said to have been founded by St Patrick. One abbot was apparently called Maucan. Porth Melgan, an inlet on St David's Head, may be named after him. Tŷ Gwyn means white or blessed house. Early graves were found here at the end of the nineteenth century. There are a variety of possible meanings of Llidi: one may be rock of the monastery, from *llu du*, the black host, but it has also been taken to mean the Vikings.[13]

Carn Llidi

Clegyr Boia

Clegyr Boia

An outcrop of Pre-Cambrian rock rises above the valley where the cathedral stands, particularly noticeable in winter when the trees are bare, and its name is Clegyr Boia (Boia's rock). In 1943, excavations revealed a Neolithic site, over which a fortified Iron Age encampment had been constructed.[14] Once, it must have been of an intimidating size and now, 1500 years later or more, stone and earth walling survives beneath bracken, gorse and bramble. Boia, Irish chieftain and druid, has a number of places named after him: Pont Clegyr Boia (bridge of Boia's rock); Ffynnon (spring) Clegyr Boia and another Iron Age fort, off Broad Haven, was known as the Rath of Boia. Castell Penlan, a motte and bailey site nearby, was also associated with him according to John Leland. A vault in the south-west corner of the Bishop's Palace was known as Vout Clegyr Boia. It led to an underground passage said to emerge at Clegyr Boia but which has been blocked for many years.

Cathedral Wells

Two wells once existed in the immediate vicinity of the cathedral and the architect Sir Gilbert Scott, during his restoration work in the nineteenth century closed up both, because streams of water running from the wells were causing an alarming undermining of the foundations of the cathedral. The streams were redirected into the River Alun along conduits opening through the wall above the ford to the west of the cathedral. A well, situated outside the east wall of the Lady Chapel, was dedicated to the Virgin Mary.[15] A second well, dedicated to St David, was believed to be in the region of the south transept. This may have been Pistyll Dewi referred to in the *Life*. In dry summers, the River Alun diminished to a trickle and the monks complained to David of the scarcity of water. David retired to a place nearby, where he spoke with his angel and, as a result, a spring of pure water gushed forth which would turn to wine for use in the Sacrament.

St David's Chapel

This was situated in the south transept of the cathedral, where relics of the saint were kept,[16] and it is also believed to be the site of the holy well. At one time it was called the Chanter's Chapel but, according to Fenton[17] it was 'more anciently and properly called St Davids Chapel, to correspond with that on the North Side, dedicated to St Andrew as both the Saints were patrons of the Church'.

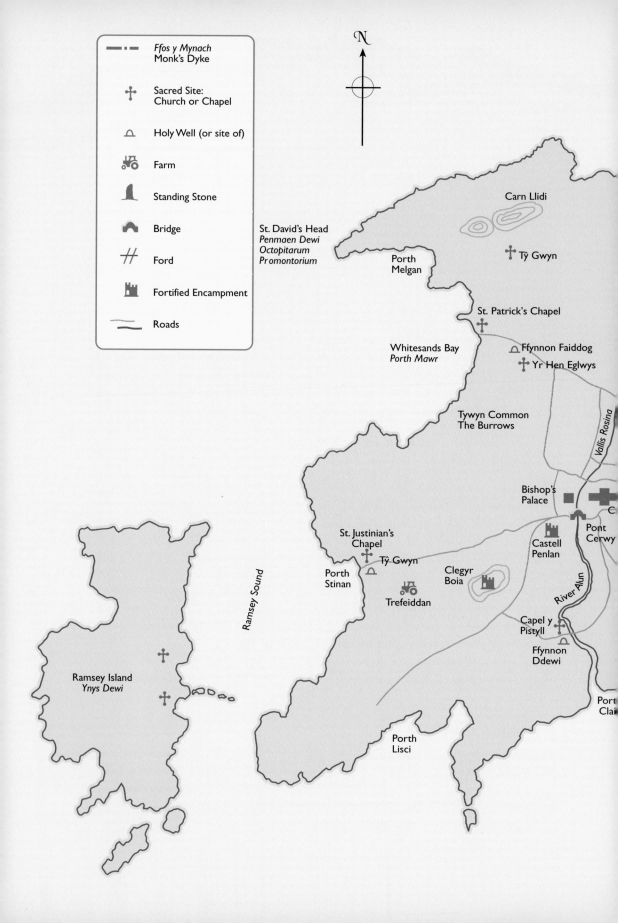

Legend

- ·—·—· *Ffos y Mynach* Monk's Dyke
- ✝ Sacred Site: Church or Chapel
- ⌂ Holy Well (or site of)
- 🚜 Farm
- ◣ Standing Stone
- ⌒ Bridge
- # Ford
- 🏰 Fortified Encampment
- ∿ Roads

N

St. David's Head
Penmaen Dewi
Octopitarum
Promontorium

Carn Llidi

✝ Tŷ Gwyn

Porth Melgan

St. Patrick's Chapel ✝

⌂ Ffynnon Faiddog
✝ Yr Hen Eglwys

Whitesands Bay
Porth Mawr

Tywyn Common
The Burrows

Vallis Rosina

Bishop's Palace

Pont Cerwy

Castell Penlan 🏰

C

St. Justinian's Chapel ✝
⌂ Tŷ Gwyn

Porth Stinan

🚜 Trefeiddan

Clegyr Boia 🏰

Ramsey Sound

River Alun

Capel y Pistyll ✝
⌂ Ffynnon Ddewi

✝ Ramsey Island
Ynys Dewi

✝

Porth Lisci

Port Clai

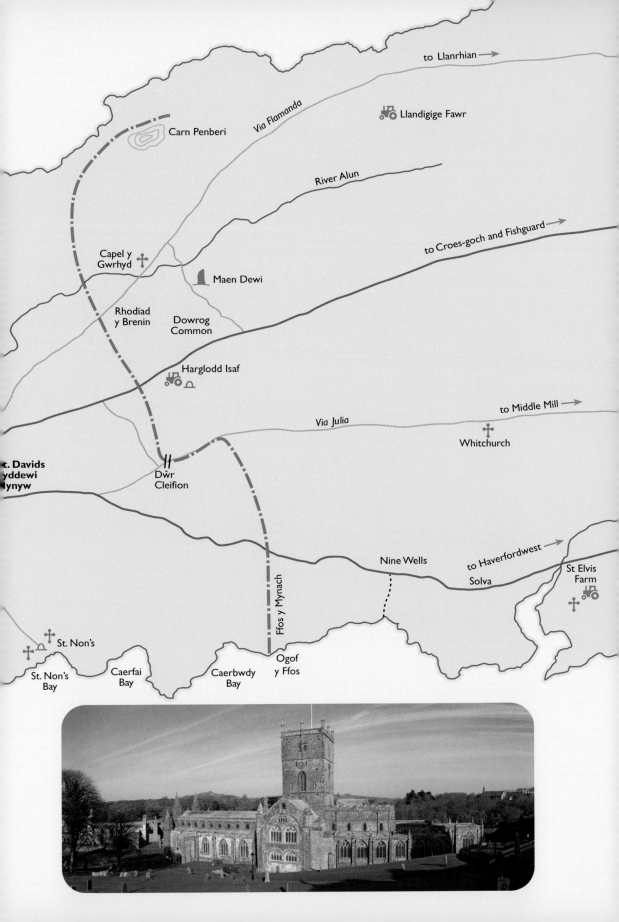

to Llanrhian →

Via Flamanda

🚜 Llandigige Fawr

Carn Penberi

River Alun

to Croes-goch and Fishguard →

Capel y
Gwrhyd ✝

Maen Dewi

Rhodiad
y Brenin

Dowrog
Common

Harglodd Isaf
🚜⌂

to Middle Mill →

Via Julia

✝
Whitchurch

t. Davids
yddewi
ynyw

Dŵr
Cleifion

Nine Wells

to Haverfordwest →

Solva

St Elvis
Farm
✝🚜

Ffos y Mynach

St. Non's
✝

✝

St. Non's
Bay

Caerfai
Bay

Caerbwdy
Bay

Ogof
y Ffos

Pont Cerwyn Dewi[18]

The Bridge of Dewi's brewing vat. In the nineteenth century the bridge was called St David's Mash Tun,[19] words derived from Middle English and medieval Latin meaning a mashing or fermenting vat. As part of the brewing process, malts would be soaked in water drawn from a natural source, in a mash tun. In the Middle Ages, it was a common practice to use beer as a mortarciser, in particular where there was a monastery or large ecclesiastical establishment, such as a Bishop's Palace, where brewing would take place on a large scale. There was a local tradition in St Davids that all the mortar used in building the cathedral was wetted with *breci* or unfermented beer instead of water.[20]

Pont Cerwyn Dewi, Merrivale

Ffos y Mynach

An ancient earthwork known as Ffos y Mynach (monk's dyke) once crossed the peninsula, from Ogof y Ffos (cave of the dyke), west of Solva, to Carn Penberi on the north coast. At this point it turned inland again to vanish near Llandigige Fawr. In a very few places, traces of earth and stone embankment can still be found. Its age is unknown, but traditions and the names of fields and farms testify to its historical existence. It is probable that it marked sanctuary land within which, according to Archdeacon Payne's account of the Ffos *c* 1825,[21] 'felons and every evil person fleeing from place to place were safe from pursuit and beyond which monks or religious persons belonging to St Davids were not permitted to go'. It is a reminder that, after the Synod of Brefi, St David was granted supreme rights of sanctuary as befitting his status as first Bishop of Western Britain. It is still possible to follow most of the course of Ffos y Mynach on a series of footpaths.

Images of St David

Very few pre-Reformation images of St David have survived. The cathedral had a wooden statue which was stolen by Irish pilgrims, but miraculously found its way back.[22] There was a painted image on his shrine in the Presbytery.[23] Three North Wales churches still have images in stained glass; Llanddeyrnog, Nercwys (two images) and Llanrhychwen, all likely to be associated with the pilgrimage from Holywell to St Davids.[24] A 'Clog Calendar'[25] of the fourteenth or fifteenth century in the Bodleian Library has a painting of the saint wearing a short tunic with his legs and feet bare. He is seated on a throne, playing a Celtic harp, wearing a bishop's mitre. It can be identified as David of Wales as it is a saint's day image, followed by St Chad on 2nd March. St David and the collect for his feast day appear in the fifteenth-century *London Hours of William Lord Hastings*.[26] A relief carving of a mother and child, in heavily-weathered sandstone 15 inches (38 cm) high, was once set into the wall of a ruined medieval chapel dedicated to St Non at Llannon in Ceredigion. It was said to be St Non with St David in her arms. It is now in the Ceredigion Museum, Aberystwyth.

All the images of St David in the cathedral are twentieth-century. The best known is the statue on the screen, dating from 1916, showing him dressed as a medieval bishop, with the dove of the Synod of Brefi on his shoulder. There is another statue in the south porch and two images in stained glass, one at the West End and the other in St Thomas's Chapel. Two scenes from the life of St David are depicted in the lower sections of the Venetian enamel mosaics by Salviati (1869),[27] which fill the lancet window spaces behind the high altar. On the left is the saint distributing bread to a mother and child. On the right, Bishops Deiniol, Paulinus, Dyfrig and David, at the Synod of Brefi, with the young child raised from the dead by David, at Dyfrig's shoulder.

The Chapel of Our Lady and St Non (St Davids) has a fine stained-glass east window (*c*1934), depicting the arrival of St Non and St David in Brittany, as well as a more stereotypical image of him with a dove on his shoulder.

A powerful and moving image in white marble carved by an Italian sculptor, Frederick Mancini in 1966, stands in the church of Llanddewi Brefi. It portrays David as an early Welsh saint, tonsured from ear to ear and dressed in rough woven cloth, with his bell and staff.[28]

Many other images exist, among them the marble statue in Cardiff City Hall by William Goscombe John (1860-1952). There is some fine stained glass by John Petts in Llanddewi Brefi Church and a beautiful image engraved on clear glass with a group of the saints on the west window of Coventry Cathedral, designed and engraved by John Hutton.

Notes

[1] Heather James, *The Cult of St David in the Middle Ages* in Martin Carver, ed., *In Search of Cult*, Woodbridge, 1993, and *Journal of Pembrokeshire Historical Society*, No 7, 1996-97.

[2] W. Rees, *An Historical Atlas of Wales from Early to Modern Times*, Faber, 1951.

[3] B. G. Charles, *Place-Names of Pembrokeshire*. National Library of Wales, 1992.

[4] J. Wyn Evans, *St Non's Chapel, St Davids, Dyfed.* HMSO, 1976; CADW *St Davids Bishop's Palace*; H. T. Payne, *Collectanea Menevensia* xci.

[5] Llannon in Ceredigion has its own parallel traditions relating to St David's birth and childhood.
J. C. Davies *Folk Lore of Mid and West Wales,* 1911, Llanerch, 1992.

[6] A tradition exists in Wales and many other countries, that any interference associated with dolmens or standing stones (such as happened when the life of St Non and her unborn child were threatened) will provoke elemental disturbance, thunder, lightning and torrential rain.

[7] Francis Green, *Pembrokeshire Parsons* West Wales Historical Records, Vol VI.

[8] Ogham was an early Irish alphabet, relating to Latin. Letters are marked by hatchings on memorial stones, often accompanied by a Latin text. They are particularly numerous in south-west Ireland.

[9] C. H. Morgan-Griffiths, *Saint Non's*.

[10] G. Middleton, *The Streets of St Davids*, Oriel Fach Press, 1977.

[11] H. T. Payne, *Collectanea Menevensia LXVII xcii*

[12] In *A Historical Tour through Pembrokeshire*, 1811, Richard Fenton quotes an old couplet 'Stinan a Devanog, Dau anwyl gymmydog' (Stinan and Devanog, two dear neighbours) and identifies him with St Dyfan of Merthyr Dyfan; H. T. Payne, *Collectanea Menevensia. XCI.*

[13] 'The Welsh called the Danes *Llu du* or the Black Army from their bearing the raven as their ensign, and such was the horror with which the natives held those pirates, that the very name was used to terrify their wayward children'. H. T. Payne, *Collectanea Menevensia* NLW 1915.

[14] A. Williams, *Clegyr Boia St Davids Excavation in 1943, Archaeologia Cambrensis*, 1952.

[15] Fenton and Jones and Freeman believe this to be Pistyll Dewi. Fenton remembered it as 'yielding water of the finest quality' but now 'choked up with rubbish'.

[16] G. C. G. Thomas, *A lost manuscript of Thomas Saint* National Library of Wales Journal XXIV, 1966.

[17] R. Fenton. *A Historical Tour Through Pembrokeshire,* 1810.

[18] G. Owen, *The Taylor's Cussion* (Facsimile), ed. E M Pritchard, 1906; also (B. G. Charles *op cit*).

[19] Pembrokeshire Archaeological Survey 1861-88,

[20] *Ibid*

[21] H. T. Payne *Collectanea Menevensia* I xcvi. Quoted and described in W. B. Jones and E. A. Freeman, *History and Antiquities of St David's.*

[22] M. J. Curley, University of Puget Sound. *Eleven Miracles of St David*, unpublished manuscript. *Traditio* Vol 62, 2007.

[23] See Ch. 3.

[24] M. Gray, *Images of Piety*. British Archaeology Reprint, Archaeo Press, 2000.

M. Lewis, *Stained Glass in North Wales up to 1850* Altrincham, 1970.

Rawlinson D 939 Bodleian reproduced in *One Hundred Saints, their lives and likenesses, drawn from Butler's Lives of the Saints and great works of Western Art.* Bullfinch Press, Littlebrown & Co., 1993. I am grateful to Mr Tristan Gray Hulse for this information.

[25] Clog Calendars were a square stick of box or other hardwood. Days of the year were represented by notches and feasts by symbols. St David's Day was represented by the saint playing on a harp, because 'he was accustomed on that instrument to praise God'. *The Book of Days: a miscellany of Popular Antiquities* ed. K. Chambers, W. and R. Chambers, 1869.

[26] Master of the First Prayer book of Maximilian Ghent, late 1470s; Janet Backhouse, *The Hastings Hours* Thames and Hudson, 1983.

P. Lord and J. Morgan-Guy, *The Visual Culture of Wales*, University of Wales Press, 2003.

[27] P. A. Robson, *The Cathedral Church of Saint David's*, Bell's Cathedral Series, 1907.

[28] The gift of Eleanor Jones, Ochrygarth Farm.

St David in History, Tradition and Folklore

S T David became a focus of Welsh identity for the early Welsh: they rallied under '*lluman glan Dewi*', the pure banner of David,[1] and in the twelfth century, the war cry of Maurice de Prendergast of Pembrokeshire was 'St David!'[2] He was much celebrated in medieval Welsh poetry:

> . . . *pob tir maith, pawb o'n iaith ni*
> *pob tuedd, pawb at Dewi.*

> [Every distant land, everyone of our language (nation)
> Every persuasion, everyone (will come) to Dewi.]

> Dafydd Llwyd ap Llywelyn ap Gruffudd (15th century)

It was enshrined in the sayings about St David, that none buried in his churchyard should go to hell:

> *A el y medrawd mynwent Dewi,*
> *Nid a yn uffern, bengwern boen.*

> [Whoever might go into the grave of the cemetery of Dewi
> Will not go to hell, quagmire of pain.]

> Gwynfardd Brycheiniog *Canu i Dewi*[3]

Although the Church ceased to celebrate the feast day of St David at the Reformation, the day on which he died, 1 March, continued to be celebrated as 'Dydd Gwyl Dewi', a secular and patriotic festival. St David's Day gained in popularity in the eighteenth and nineteenth centuries and has been celebrated with fervour right up to the present day.

Leek or Daffodil?

On this day, the leek (*y genhinen*) has always been worn as a national emblem.[4] The tradition of the leek as the authentic Welsh emblem is ascribed to St David, who was said to have ordered that it should be worn to identify the (subsequently victorious) Welsh in an early battle with the Saxons.

The seventeenth-century poet Michael Drayton wrote in *Polyolbion* (1622) that David

> Did so trulie fast,
> As he did onelie drinke what crystall Hodney[5] yeelds,
> And fed upon the Leeks he gather'd in the fields.
> In memory of whom, in the revolving yere
> The Welch-men on his day that sacred herbe doe weare.

The leek's colours, green and white, were Welsh royal colours and although it was not part of the staple diet the leek had the attributes of a sacred plant. Growing leeks in the garden brought luck and kept away evil spirits. The leek was a symbol of purity and immortality and furnished a protection against lightning. Rubbing the body with leeks protected soldiers in battle. The Welsh Guards wear a leek as a cap badge and the Royal Welch Regiment maintains a St David's Day tradition of the youngest recruit having to eat a raw leek at the St David's Day dinner. In Shakespeare's play, *Henry V*, the king states that he wears a leek on St David's day 'For a memorable honour, for I am Welsh, you know'.[6]

St David's Day is marked by religious services, celebration dinners and eisteddfodau (cultural festivals). Children wearing Welsh traditional costume and either a leek or a daffodil, celebrate the day with services and eisteddfodau. The daffodil became a popular emblem in the nineteenth century and Welsh names for it include *blodau Dewi* (Dewi's flowers) and *cennin Dewi* (Dewi's leek). It was promoted by David Lloyd George who caused it to be used in preference to the leek at the Investiture of the Prince of Wales in 1911.

Folklore of the year's turning

St David's Day is followed by the feast day of St Chad and these festivals marked the time when oats and barley, peas and beans should be sown. In Cwm Gwaun, Pembrokeshire, where it was customary to follow the Julian Calendar, 'Old St David's Day' on 12th March was marked by placing a *cannwyll pren* – wooden candle – instead of a tallow one in the candlestick on the table. Candles were a scarce commodity and as the evenings began to draw out, supping by candlelight for the farmhands was over till the autumn.

Nos dwgwl Ddewi fe gaiff Ben,
Fita swper gida'r ganwyll bren

It ends on Dewi's Feast-day night,
Eat supper by wooden candle-light.[7]

Pan ddaw Dewi ar farch gwyn,
Fe ddaw Mair ar fuwch goch.

When St David comes in on a white horse,
Mary will come in on a red cow.[8]

(When St David's Day is rough, Lady Day, 25th March, Feast of the
Assumption, will be fair – the equivalent of the belief that when
March comes in like a lion, it will go out like a lamb.)

Mae'r dydd yn ymestyn
Gam ceiliog Dydd Nadolig,
Awr gyfan hen Ddydd Calan,
Dwy awr hir Dygwyl Fair*
Dros ben cyfri Dygwyl Ddewi.[9]

The year stretches –
On Christmas Day, the step of a cockerel
Old New Year's Day, a whole hour
Mary's Feast Day* two hours longer
Dewi's Feast Day, too many to count.

Translation Anona Gray.

(*Candlemas, 2 February).

Corpse Candle – Cannwyll Gorff [10]

St David is said to have asked that some sign might be given of a coming death,
so that the dying should not go to the grave unshriven, but that they might
repent and be assured of eternal life. Hence the old Welsh belief in the Corpse
Candle: this is a will-o-the-wisp light that is seen to precede a death, hovering
over the path that the coffin will take from house to cemetery.

St David and the natural world

One of the characteristics of the saints of the Celtic lands was their feeling of
closeness and fellowship with the natural world. St David sent a swarm of bees
to Ireland with their beekeeper, St Modomnoc, admonishing them not to return

Maen Dewi standing stone

to his monastery.[11] According to George Owen[12] of Henllys, St David was so entranced by the beauty of the nightingale's song, and such was his distraction from prayer, that he prayed that the bird might never again sing in his diocese. This is nearly true! The nightingale is a vagrant; it may settle for a while and sing, but does not breed in the western areas of Wales. The last recorded song in the St David area was in Pointz Castle, near Solva, in 1948, but the singing bird is rare in Pembrokeshire. Giraldus Cambrensis remarked that the nightingale was never seen in Wales.[13]

Sacred Stones

Many legends and sacred stones dedicated to St David still survive in south Wales. They are found on sites which have close associations with him, in Llannon, Henfynyw and Llanddewi Brefi, all in Ceredigion; also in Gower and south-east Wales. These are outside the small area covered by this book.

East of St. Davids, a large standing stone on the Dowrog Common is called Maen Dewi (David's stone) and a farm nearby was known as Tir (land) Maen Dewi. Another stone known as Maen Dewi stood in Whitchurch.[14] A ring cross associated with St David is Mesur y Dorth, set into a wall a mile from Croesgoch towards Fishguard. The Welsh translates as 'measure of the loaf'. In time of scarcity, David, and subsequently the bishops of St Davids, decreed that loaves should be baked no bigger than the circle. In later times, it was at this point that pilgrims journeying to St Davids from the north (probably *via* Nevern), are said to have taken their last meal before reaching the Cathedral.[15] There may have been more than one such stone: according to Cathedral records, in 1847 a request was received for the removal of 'a gatepost called Mesurydorth, on which there is an ancient inscription at Pen Arthur farm', about half a mile from the Cathedral. This stone is now in the Lapidarium and is known as the Gurmarc stone, after the name carved on it.

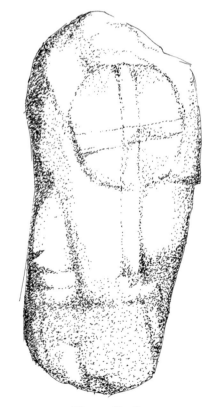

Mesur y Dorth

St David's Head

St David's Diamonds

These are fine quartz crystals which used to be found in a vein of quartz in Ogof Crystal (Crystal Cave), on the north side of St David's Head. The seam is now exhausted and access to this site is difficult and dangerous.

St David's Bell

The use of bells in religious ritual comes from the east and predates Christianity by thousands of years. Bells had a threefold use, in calling the attention of the deity, banishing evil spirits and protecting the priest from the power of the deity. The early saints inherited this traditional use of the bell from Christian hermits and small monastic communities in Egypt. These early Celtic handbells were made of riveted iron plates, bore names and had magical powers. They were held in superstitious awe and oaths were taken on them. Some are still in existence.

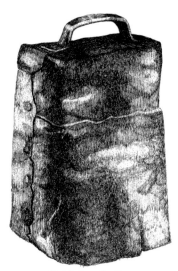

Celtic handbell

According to Giraldus Cambrensis, St David's bell was called Bangu[16] (the dear loud one) and was held in the church at Glascwm in the old county of Radnor.

Holy Wells

Apart from the wells already mentioned, Francis Jones gives a comprehensive list of holy wells dedicated to St David in his book *The Holy Wells of Wales*. Ffynnonddewi, near Brawdy, was visited by pilgrims on their way to St Davids. Another of the same name, to the east of St Davids, existed in 1765, but has now been lost. Harglodd Isaf Farm also had a holy well dedicated to the saint, recorded in 1669. A well dedicated to St David was believed to have been situated inside the Cathedral in the vicinity of the South Transept, once known as St David's Chapel.

St David and his fellow saints

In the fifth and sixth centuries, there were numerous men and some women who dedicated their lives to God, living as hermits or in small monastic communities in western Britain. They became the early native saints and have churches and other sites dedicated to them. In Wales, these sites usually bear the saint's name, prefixed by *Llan*, originally meaning an enclosure, but later denoting a church. On the Dewisland peninsula, four saints who feature in the *Life* have places dedicated to them: Padrig (Patrick), Aeddan Maeddog (Aidan), Teilo and Aelfyw (Elvis). St David features in the medieval *Life* of St Stinan (Justinan) and according to tradition St Brynach of Nevern was a close friend of St David.

St Patrick/Padrig[17]

According to the *Life* of St David, St Patrick, patron saint of Ireland, came first to Ceredigion and then to Demetia[18] (Dyfed), intending to set up his monastery in Vallis Rosina (the Valley). He was told by an angel, however, that the place was reserved for one who would come in thirty years' time. Patrick was angry and disappointed but the angel showed him 'the whole of the island of Ireland' from the seat which is in Vallis Rosina which is now named 'the Seat of Patrick'.[19] The remains of St Patrick's medieval Chapel are at Whitesands where a heavily-lichened marble plaque on a mound on the north side of the beach marks the site.[20] A rock outcrop on Croeswdig land is called Carn Padrig and the southern gateway through the perimeter wall of the Cathedral is called 'Porth Padrig' (Patrick's Gate). Llech Lafar the 'Talking Stone' that once spanned the River Alun near the cathedral and was famous for crying out whenever a corpse was carried across it, also had some link with St Patrick:

Edewis Padric drwy dic dagreu,
Lloneid Llech Llauar, hygar hygleu
Pan aeth Ywerton y wyrth ynteu,
Ac Eigyl racda, dra dra thonneu . . .

Patrick left with angry tears,
The fill of the dear audible Llech Lafar,
When his miracle went to Ireland,
With angels before him, away across the waves...

'Canu i Dewi' ('Poem to Dewi'), Gwynfardd Brycheiniog[21]

Patrick was also one of the three saints whose images appeared with that of St David on his medieval shrine in the presbytery of the cathedral.[22]

St Justinian's Chapel

St Stinan[23]

St Stinan, the Latinised form of Justinian, was a Breton who made his home on Ramsey Island. He became a close friend of David and eventually his confessor. A local legend describes how Stinan became disgusted at the laxness of David's monastery and, in a bid for isolation, made an island of Ramsey by hacking it away from the mainland with an axe. As he hacked, the axe became blunter and the pieces (now called 'The Bitches') larger. The last and biggest is called the Axe. His extreme asceticism became too much for his followers and they killed him on the island, cutting off his head. Undaunted, the diminutive Breton picked up his head and crossed the Sound with it under his arm, setting it down at the top of the cliff. The spring that rose from the earth is marked today by a holy well. Close by is the chapel dedicated to the saint and within its walls is a square marked by stone footings – possibly the site of the saint's grave chapel.[24] His remains appear to have been removed to the cathedral at some point. At the end of the 15th century, William Worcestre said that St Stinan 'lies in a chapel in the church of St David *sub ejus tumba*, under, or below, his tomb'.[25] There are only two other dedications to St Stinan in the county, at Llanstinan and Freystrop.

Holy Well,
St Justinian's

St Aeddan[26]

St Aeddan was a young disciple of David when the saint founded his monastery. His full name was Aeddan Maeddog and both names exist in Pembrokeshire. On the peninsula, a farm and a well are named after him: Trefeiddan and Ffynnon Faiddog. Llawhaden church is dedicated to him. He became Bishop of Ferns, Ireland, but never forgot his devotion to David. In Irish tradition, David died in Aeddan's arms.

Trefeiddan farm

St Brynach[27]

St Brynach, an Irishman who lived in Nevern, was another close friend of David. A legend connects St David with the Nevern High Cross.[28] David was carrying a beautifully carved stone cross up to Llanddewi Brefi, as a memorial to himself. On the way, he called at Nevern (Nanhyfer) to see Brynach and was persuaded by his friend to leave the cross there. The carved wheel-headed cross in the churchyard is 11th-century and though not the cross of the story, it could have 'inherited' a tradition. The story is also a reminder that Nevern was the last stop for the medieval pilgrims who travelled from Llanddewi Brefi to St Davids, along the ancient pilgrim routes.

Nevern High Cross

St Teilo[29] and St Aelfyw[30] (St Elvis Farm, Solva)

St Aelfyw (Elvis), cousin to St David and Bishop of Munster in Ireland, baptised David at Porth Clais. Two places near Solva bear his name: a house – Fagwr Eilw (enclosure of Eilw) and St Elvis Farm. On the same site there was a church dedicated to Teilo, a disciple of St David and a later bishop of Mynyw, whose local cult area is in south Pembrokeshire. In 1944, foundations of the church were still visible and many ancient graves were discovered on the site.[31]

St Ismael/Ysfael[32]

St Ismael was present at the founding of St David's monastery; churches dedicated to him are in south Pembrokeshire.

The Jerusalem Altar

The portable altar which St David received from the Patriarch, on his pilgrimage to Jerusalem, was taken by an angel to his church at Llangyfelach, near Swansea. The altar was described as being 'potent in innumerable miracles' and

44

after the saint's death was kept covered in skins, being too holy for mortal eyes. The stone altar set into the table in the South Transept acquired the reputation in the twentieth century of being that altar, but this is unlikely.

Mystery Play, *Buchez Santes Non* (Life of St Non)

A Breton medieval mystery play told the story of St Non and St David. It dates from before the twelfth century and the text is fourteenth century. The original manuscript is in Paris and a photocopy of parts of this, a translation and the new edition are held in the Cathedral Library.

The devil's footprints

On the south side of the Cathedral is a flat grave slab (nineteenth-century) with two curious indentations. They are known as the devil's footprints, left where he landed, when he attempted to fight with St David on the roof of the Cathedral, but was pushed off by the saint.

Britain's smallest city

St Davids has always been recognised as a city because it has a cathedral, the seat (see) of the bishop. In 1995, the Queen granted the city its Charter. It is Britain's smallest city, the original 'city' being contained within the medieval perimeter wall of the cathedral close. St Davids' further claim to metropolitan status, that is, to be the throne of the Archbishop of Wales and independent of Canterbury, was strongly upheld by Giraldus Cambrensis (1146-1223). Independence from Canterbury was finally achieved in 1920 when the Welsh Church was disestablished.[33]

St Davids is the only British cathedral where the sovereign is a member of the cathedral Chapter. The sovereign's stall in the choir is the First Cursal and above the seat is the Royal Coat of Arms. Before the Reformation it may have been occupied by the Master of St Mary's College of Priests and was worth £1 a year, but it was then given to Henry VIII. There is an old tradition that it was granted to Richard I on his return from the Crusades,[34] however H. T. Payne regarded Edward I as the first Royal Prebendary.[35]

The first of the Triads of the Isle of Britain, which was probably a medieval addition to older material, refers to Dewi as Chief Bishop of Mynyw:

> *Dewi yn Pen Ysgyb ym Mynyv*[36]

Geoffrey of Monmouth in his *History of the Kings of Britain* writes of Merlin's prophecy that

> Menevia shall bear the pall of the City of Legions[37]

The smallest city in Britain.

A pall, or pallium, forms part of a bishop's vestments and is a symbol of his authority. Traditionally, when Dyfrig (Dubricius) Archbishop of Caerleon (City of Legions) retired to end his days on Ynys Enlli (Bardsey Island), he created David archbishop in his place. David then removed the see to Menevia, thus fulfilling the prophecy.

St David's status was enhanced further when he was consecrated archbishop by the Patriarch in Jerusalem. The Synod of Brefi, confirmed by the later Synod of Victory, made David first among the Bishops of Western Britain.

Notes

1 *Armes Prydein c.* 930. ed. Rachel Bromwich, University of Wales Press, 1972.

2 Baring Gould and Fisher, *Lives of the British Saints II*, 1907.

3 M. E. Owen, 'Prolegomena to a study of the historical context of Gwynfardd Brycheiniog's "Poem to Dewi".' *Studia Celtica* Vol 26/27, 1991-92.

4 J. C. Davies, *Folklore of West and Mid-Wales*, 1911, facsimile reprint, Llanerch, 1992.

5 Hoddnant, or fair valley, where the cathedral stands.

6 Henry V, born in Monmouth 1387, known as Henry of Monmouth.

7 W. Meredith Morris 51-52 *A Glossary of the Demetian Dialect*, 1910. Llanerch 1991. The author also records the use of the oath *Men Dewi wyn*, By the Holy St David, often shortened to *Dewin*, within his memory. I am grateful to Anona Gray for her translation of the verse.

8 W. Meredith Morris, *op cit.*

9 J. C. Davies, *op cit*; T. Jones *Ar Dafod Gwerin*, Cymdeithas Lyfrau Ceredigion (reference to William Rhys Jones 1868-87); Gwenith Gwyn, NLW MS 1283.

10 J. C. Davies, *ibid.*

11 J. C. Davies, *ibid.*

12 George Owen, *Description of Pembrokeshire* ed. Dillwyn Miles, Gomer Press, 1994; J. C. Davies *op. cit.*

13 Giraldus Cambrensis, *Journey through Wales*, Penguin, 1978.

14 'Immediately in front of the churchyard gate, on the margin of an open common. The stone was described as '22 inches across above the soil and 19 inches in breadth . . . probably the stump of a cross or part of a calvary . . . in former times all bodies were carried round this stone before entering the church.' RCAM Whitchurch.

15 Richard Fenton, *A Historical Tour through Pembrokeshire*, 1810.

16 *Bangu* was also the pre-Reformation name for the corpse bell, kept in all Welsh Churches, taken to the house of the deceased and sounded on the way to the church. J. C. Davies *op cit.*

17 Baring Gould and Fisher, *Lives of the British Saints*, Vol. IV, London 1907

18 W. Rees, Plate 22 *An Historical Atlas of Wales from early to modern times*, Faber, 1954.

19 *Life of St David*, A stone seat set into the gateway of The Treasury in the cathedral close is known as St Patrick's seat. In official literature it is described as a porter's seat.

20 St Patrick's Chapel was excavated in 1924. *Archaeologia Cambrensis*, 1925; H. T. Payne, *Collectanea Menevensia* (LXVII) xcii.

21 M. E. Owen, *Prolegomena. op. cit.*

22 '. . . St David's Shrine . . . St David himself is painted in his Pontificalibus; and on each side of him is a Bishop Saint, one by the inscription is known to be St Patrick; the other is somewhat defac'd', Browne Willis, *Survey of the Cathedral Church of St Davids*, 1717.

23 S. Baring Gould and J. Fisher *Lives of the British Saints* Vol III, 1907; *Life of St Justinan* (NB not Justinian as is commonly spelt) John of Tynemouth, *Nova Legenda Angliae*, ed. C. Horstman, Oxford, 1901; *Life of St David* A. W. Wade-Evans, SPCK, 1923.

24 The site was excavated in 1924. *Archaeologia Cambrensis* Vol LXXX1.

25 W. B. Jones and E. A. Freeman, *History and Antiquities of St Davids*, 1856

26 *Life of St Aidan. Vita Sanctorum Hiberniae*, Charles Plummer, 1910; A. W. Wade-Evans *Life of St David*, 1923.

27 *Life of St Brynach* ed. A. W. Wade-Evans, *Vitae Sanctorum Britanniae et Genealogiae*, 1944.

28 J. C. Davies, *op. cit.*

29 *Life of St Teilo*, Book of Llandaf, J. Gwenogvryn Evans; *The Text of the Book of Llan Dav*, Oxford, 1893.

30 *Life of St Aelfyw, Acta Sanctorum Hiberniae*, eds. De Smedt and De Backer, 1888.

31 Parish of St Elvies, 1034 RCAM 1925.

[32] S. Baring Gould and J. Fisher *Lives of the British Saints* Vol III, London 1907.

[33] The Archbishop of Wales is elected from among the Welsh bishops but does not reside in St Davids.

[34] Henry Evans, *Tŵr-y-felin History and Guide to St Davids* 1923.

[35] H. T. Payne, 107 *Collectanea Menevensia* NLW SD/CH/B, 1815.

[36] *Trioedd Ynys Prydein, The Welsh Triads*

[37] Geoffrey of Monmouth, *History of the Kings of Britain* Penguin Classics, 1988.

Epilogue

SAINT DAVID gave his life to God and humanity; he gave his name to a place, where his presence is still felt by thousands who come to his shrine, and his legend to Wales. His last words were:

Frodyr a chwiorydd, byddwch lawen a chedwch eich ffydd a'ch cred, a gwnewch y pethau bychain a glywsoch ac a welsoch gennyf fi.

(Brothers and sisters, be cheerful and keep your faith and belief, and do the little things that you have heard and seen through me.)

Welsh Life of St David

These words bring him close to those who seek him, and although 1,400 years have passed since Dewi Sant walked on Welsh soil, his land remains a focus of pilgrimage – remote, mysterious and holy.

Nave ceiling

Trwyn Hwrddyn

Bibliography

Annales Cambriae (Harleian). J. Ingram. *The Anglo Saxon Chronicle*, 1912

Archaeologia Cambrensis

Bartrum, P. C. *A Welsh Classical Dictionary, People in History and Legend up to about AD 1000*, National Library of Wales, 1993

Baring Gould, S. and Fisher, J. *Lives of the British Saints*, 1907

Bell's Cathedral Series *Saint David's, the Cathedral and See*, 1901

Black Book of St Davids *Cymmrodorion Record Series No. 5*, 1902

Bowen, E. G. *Dewi Sant, Saint David* University of Wales Press, 1961

Browne, L. Willis *Survey of the Cathedral Church of St Davids*, 1717

Chadwick, N. et al. *Studies in Early British History*, 1954

Charles, B. G. *The Place Names of Pembrokeshire* National Library of Wales, 1992

Cowley, F. G. *A note on the discovery of St David's Body* British Board of Celtic Studies, 1960

Crowley, D. *St David of Wales* Catholic Truth Society B 414, 1965

Davies, W. *Wales in the Early Middle Ages* Leicester University Press, 1982

Dumville, D. N. *Saint David of Wales: Kathleen Hughes Memorial Lectures on Mediaeval Welsh History*, University of Cambridge, 2001

Edwards, O. T. *Matins, Lauds and Vespers for St David's Day: the mediaeval Office of the Welsh Patron Saint* NLW MS 20541E. D. S. Brewer, Cambridge, 1990

Evans D. Simon, *The Welsh Life of St David* University of Wales Press, 1988

Evans, J. W. and Turner, R. *St Davids Bishop's Palace, St Non's Chapel. St Davids Bishop's Palace, St Non's Chapel*, CADW

Evans, J. W. and Worsley, R. *St Davids Cathedral 1181-1981* Yr Oriel Fach Press, 1981

Evans, J. W. and Wooding, Jonathan M. eds., 'St David of Wales: Cult, Church and Nation', *Studies in Celtic History* Boydell, 2007

Evans, H. *Twr-y-Felin History and Guide to St Davids* 1923

Evans, K. M. *Saint David, Dewi Sant* SPCK, 1957

Fenton, R. *A Historical Tour through Pembrokeshire* Dyfed County Council, 1994

Giraldus Cambrensis *The Itinerary through Wales and the Description of Wales* Penguin, 1978

Harris, S. H. *Saint David in the Liturgy* Cardiff University Press, 1940

Henken, E. *Traditions of the Welsh Saints* D S Brewer, 1987

Hughes, K. *Celtic Britain in the Early Middle Ages: Studies in Scottish and Welsh Sources* ('Holy Men of the Welsh'), Woodbridge, 1980

James, D. W. *St David's and Dewisland* University of Wales Press, 1981

James, H. 'The Cult of St David in the Middle Ages' Martin Carver, ed., *In Search of Cult*, Woodbridge, 1993; *Journal of Pembrokeshire Historical Society*, No 7, 1996-97

James J. W. *Rhygyfarch's Life of St David* University of Wales Press, 1983

John, T. and Rees, N. *Pilgrimage, a Welsh Perspective* Gomer Press, 2002

Jones, F. *The Holy Wells of Wales* University of Wales, 1954

Jones, T. *Brut y Tywysogion* (Peniarth MS 20) University of Wales Press, 1952

Jones W. B. and Freeman, E A. *History and Antiquities of St Davids* Pembrokeshire County Council Cultural Services, 1998

Middleton, G. W. *The Streets of St Davids* Oriel Fach Press, 1977

Nash Williams, V. E. *The Early Christian Monuments of Wales* University of Wales Press, 1949

Owen, G. *Description of Pembrokeshire* ed. Dillwyn Miles, Gomer Press, 1994

Payne, H. T. *Collectanea Menevensia* NLW SD/CH/B, 1815

Rees, N. *The Mediaeval Shrines of St Davids Cathedral, St David and St Caradog*, St Davids Cathedral, 1998

Roberts, E. P. *Dewi Sant Friends of St Davids Cathedral Report*, 1990

Royal Commission on Ancient Monuments, Pembrokeshire, 1925

Stephens, M. *The New Companion to the Literature of Wales* University of Wales Press, 1998

Wade-Evans, A. W. *Life of St David*, S.P.C.K.,1923

Williams, G. 'The Tradition of St David in Wales', *Links with the past; Swansea and Brecon historical essays* Christopher Davies, 1974

Index

Altarnon 7
Alun river 7, 8, 21, 27
Armes Prydein Fawr 35
Arthur 3
Asser 13

Bangu 41
Bardsey (see Ynys Enlli) 46
Barlow (Bishop) 17
Bees 4
Boia 7, 8, 25, 27
Brandivy 7
Brittany 3, 7, 24, 31
Broad Haven 27
Browne Willis 22, 51
Buchez Santes Non 45
Burnet rose 17
Burrows, the 25

Caerforiog 24
Caerleon 45-6
Callistus II (Pope) 14
Canterbury 33
Cannwyll Gorff 37
Capel y Gwrhyd 24-5
Capel y Pistyll 23
Carbon dating 17
Carmarthenshire 21
Carn Llidi 26
Carn Penberi 30
Castell Penlan 27
Catalogue of the Saints of
    Ireland 13
Ceredig 3
Ceredigion 4, 21, 31, 39, 41
Chapel of Our Lady and St
    Non 24
Chapel of the Fathom (see
    Capel y Gwrhyd) 25
Chapel, Holy Trinity 17
Chichele (Archbishop) 17
Cille Muine 7, 21
City (status) 45
Clas 21
Clegyr Boia 7, 25, 27
Clerkes of Oxenford 19 note 23
Climate 7
Clog Calendar 31
Coat of Arms 17, 18
Cornwall 3
Corpse Candle (see Cannwyll
    Gorff) 37
Coventry Cathedral 32

Croesgoch 39
Cross-inscribed stones 39
Cunedda 3
Cynir 3, 5

Daffodil 35-6
Dafydd Llwyd ap Llywelyn ap
    Gruffudd 35
Davidstowe 7
Deisi 21
Demetia 41
Devil's footprints 45
Devon 7
Dewisland 18, 21
Dewstowe 7
Dirinon 7
Dove 11
Dowrog Common 39
Drayton, Michael 36
Druid(s) 37
Dunod 8
Dydd Gwyl Ddewi 35
Dyfed 21
Dyfrwr 1

Eglwys – yr hen 25
Edward I 14, 45
Eleanor (Queen) 14
Ewenni (Prior of) 15
Evangelium 13

Fenton, Richard 27
Ferrar (Bishop) 17
Ffos y Mynach 30-1
Ffynnon Clegyr Boia 27
Ffynnon Ddewi 11, 41
Ffynnon Faiddog 43
Fishguard 21, 39

Geoffey of Monmouth 45
Gifts (to David) 9
Giraldus Cambrensis 45
Glascwm 7
Glastonbury 7, 13, 15
Glyn Rhosyn 7, 21
Gower 39
Gruffudd ap Cynan 15
Gurmarc stone 39
Gustilianus 6
Gwynfardd Brycheiniog 13, 35

Harglodd Isaf 41
Henry II 14

Henry V 36
Henry VIII 45
Henfynyw 6, 39
Hoddnant 21
Holy water stoup 25
Holy wells 1
Human sacrifice 12 note 12
Hutton, John 32

Idnert filius Jacobi 13
Ieuan ap Rhydderch 5
Ireland 2, 4, 7
Iolo Goch 4

Jerusalem 9, 14, 44
John de Gamages 15
John, William Goscombe 32

Lady Chapel 27
Language (Welsh) 2
Leland, John 25
Leek 35-6
Leominster 7
Lhuyd, Edward 13
Liber Davidis 13
Life of St David 17
Lindow Moss 12 note 12
Lisci 8, 25

Llanbadarn Fawr 3
Llanddeyrnog 31
Llanrhychwen 31
Llanddewi Brefi 3, 9, 13, 31-2,
    39, 44
Llandigige Fawr 21
Llangyfelach 7, 44
Llanon (Pembs) 23
Llannon (Ceredigion) 31, 39
Llawhaden 43
London Hours of William,
    Lord Hastings 31
Lotivy 7

Maen Dewi 39
Mancini, Frederick 9, 31
Mappa Mundi 14
Martyrology of Tallaght 13
Maucan 4, 26
Maurice de Prendergast 35
Menevia 14, 21
Merlin 3, 4
Merrivale 30
Mesur y Dorth 39

Movi 5
Mynydd Carn 15
Mynyw 1, 4, 7, 21, 44

National Library of Wales,
	Aberystwyth 17
Nevern 39, 44
Nerquis 31
Newgale 21
Nightingale 39
Nun Street 23

Ogham 23
Orthodox Church 17
Octopitarum Promontorium 26
Owain Tudor 17

Palace, Bishop's 18, 27, 30
Payne, Archdeacon 30
Pebidiog 18, 21
Pelagius 9
Pembrokeshire 21
Pen Arthur Farm 39
Pen Pont Antiphoner 17
Peter de Leia (Bishop) 13
Petts, John 32
Pilgrims, Pilgrimage 14, 23,
	39, 41, 44
Pilgrim paths 21
Pistyll 23, 27
Plague 7
Pointz Castle 39
Pont Cerwyn Dewi 30
Porth Clais 21, 23, 44
Porth Lisci 8, 25
Porth Mawr 4, 21
Porth Melgan 26
Prophecy 3, 45
Ptolemy 26

Quartz crystals 40

Ramsey Island 22, 26, 42
Reception Chapels 24
Reformation 13, 17, 23
Relics 15, 17, 27, 19 note 18
Reliquary 17

Repton 7
Rhodiad y Brenin 2, 25
Rhygyfarch 3, 8, 14, 18
Rhys ap Tewdwr 15, 17
Richard I 45
Richard II 14
Richard de Carew (Bishop) 15
Rome 9, 14
Royal Welch Regiment 36

Saint Aeddan 7, 41, 43
	Aelfyw (Elvis) 4, 5, 41, 44
	Andrew 14
	Brynach 41, 44
	Cadoc 13
	Chad 31, 36
	Deiniol 10, 31
	Docus (see Cadoc)
	Dubricius (see Dyfrig)
	Dyfrig 10, 31
	Gildas 4, 13
	Ismael 7, 44
	Justinian (see Stinan)
	Maeddog (see Aeddan)
	Modomnoc 37
	Non 3, 4, 7, 22, 24, 31, 45
	Padarn 9
	Patrick (Padrig) 3, 4, 15,
		26, 41-2
	Paulinus 6, 10, 31
	Stinan 15, 26, 41, 42-3
	Teilo 10, 41, 44
St Aidan's Church 43
St David's Altar 44
St David's Bell 40
St David's Chapel 41
St David's Churchyard 35
St David's Diamonds 40
St David's Day (see Dydd
	Gwyl Ddewi) 35
St David's Head 26, 40
St David's Shrine 42
St Divy 7
St Elvis Farm 44
St Justinian's 42-3
St Non's 22-3
Salmon 4

Salisbury Psalter 13
Salviati 31
Sanctuary (rights of) 9
Sant 3, 4
Satrapa 8
Scott, Sir Gilbert 27
Solva 30
Stag 4
Standing stones 4-5
Sulien (Bishop) 3
Synod of Brefi 11, 31
Synod of Victory 11, 46

Teifi 4
Tollund 12 note 12
Treasures 4
Trioedd Ynys Prydein 9
Triads 9, 45
Tyddewi 1, 21
Tŷ Gwyn 4, 26
Tywyn Common 7, 25

Valley of Roses 21
Vallis Rosina 7, 21, 41
Viking raids 15
Vikings 26

Walden, Roger (Archbishop of
	Canterbury) 17
Watercress 1
Waterman 1
Welsh Guards 36
Welsh royal colours 36
Whitchurch 39
Whitesands 4, 7, 21, 25, 41
Whitland 6
William Morris School 24
William I 14
Wine 27
Wulstan, David 19 note 23

Yellow Pestilence 7
Ynys Dewi 22, 26
Ynys Enlli 46
Ynys Tyfanog 26

Ring Cross Stone, St Non's.